P9-DNU-827

Contents

About the Author

Amy Barickman is considered a leader in the sewing and craft pattern design industry. After graduating from the University of Kansas with a degree in art and design, she founded Indygo Junction in 1990 to publish and market books and patterns designed by fresh, new talent. Amy's vision for anticipating popular trends has led her to discover artists and guide them to create with innovative materials and tools. With a keen eye for new market opportunities, Amy spotted the emerging vintage art movement and began an impressive archive of vintage ephemera. As technology improved, she envisioned what crafters could be with their home computer and printer. She founded The Vintage Workshop in 2002 to create products that combine timeless vintage artwork with the computer and inkjet printable materials. Her designs use downloads of digitized vintage artwork from her website and from CDs that she developed from her large archive collections.

Amy has identified and marketed more than 25 designers, published 600 pattern titles, 70 books, and has licensed her fabric line to Red Rooster. Her most recent books are Yo-Yo Fashions, Denim Redesign, Needlefelted Fashions and Needlefelted Accessories. For a complete book listing, visit the websites listed below. She inspires countless crafters to awaken their own creative spirit and experiment with the newest sewing, fabric and crafting techniques.

Amy Barickman's work has been featured in several magazines, including the recent honor of being named one of Country Living magazine's Women Entrepreneurs "Celebration of Creativity." She has made television appearances on HGTV, America Quilts, and Sewing with Nancy.

{ For all the latest news, subscribe to our newsletters at www.indygojunction.com and www.thevintageworkshop.com. }

button{ware}

[bŭtń•wăř]: the art of making creative adornments and embellishments

by Amy Barickman

INDYGO JUNCTION
Handmade Style for the Creative Spirit

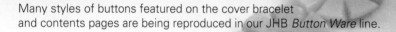

Many styles of buttons featured on the cover bracelet
and contents pages are being reproduced in our JHB *Button Ware* line.

For a complete listing of acknowledgments and credits see page 79.

Published by Indygo Junction
P.O. Box 30238
Kansas City, MO 64112
913-341-5559
www.indygojunction.com

Library of Congress Control Number: 2008924206

ISBN 10:0-9754918-4-9
ISBN 13:978-0-9754918-4-3

Introduction

Button collecting is one of my favorite creative addictions. I find endless satisfaction in sorting through buttons and discovering the ones I can't live without. My attraction to these vintage embellishments led me to pursue publishing this book. To make the reproduction of these designs more accessible, we partnered with JHB International to create the projects using their current collection of colorful and stylish buttons. Our companies hope that it will provide crafters with a wonderful guide to using buttons to create unique and eye-catching jewelry.

JHB International began when Mrs. Jean Howard Barr, of Denver, Colorado, was preparing to leave on a European buying trip for her family business. A knitting store asked her to bring back a specific type of metal button for use on sweaters. From this modest request, the company has grown to become one of the world's major suppliers of basic, novelty and fashion buttons.

Creativity was a founding cornerstone of JHB, and the company remains dedicated to innovation. Together we are designing affordable *Button Ware* kits that provide crafters with a one-stop shopping approach for creating beautiful accessories. The kits include everything you need to make your very own piece from the direction sheet to the jump ring.

{ *Sorting through vintage button cards at flea markets is a great source of inspiration.* }

Also look for our *Button Ware* line of reproduction vintage buttons. Whether you are searching for vintage or contemporary buttons, the hunt can be a fun and exciting part of the creative process. One person I know started the search by going through her grandmother's attic. Vintage buttons are also easily found in flea markets, at garage sales, and on Ebay. In choosing which button to buy, my advice is this: Express yourself! Buy what you like and eventually it will find its way into a design. Use this book as your guide to create inspiring designs with your favorite buttons.

{ *If life is too hectic for the hunt, try one of the companion kits we developed for designs found in this book.* }

Something is magical about buttons. They are commonplace; you see them everywhere in every size, shape, and color and you tend to take them for granted. But, in fact, buttons can be the crowning glory of any good fashion statement. In fact, if you look back centuries, back to their origin around

conceivable material— metal, glass, plastic, rubber, cloth, wood. . . you name it, someone has made a button out of it. Mother-of-pearl buttons have been popular for centuries, dating to sixteenth century Europe and named during the reign of Queen Elizabeth the First. Later, Queen Victoria started a button

Tools

2000 B.C., buttons started appearing for decorative purposes only. The buttonhole was not invented until the thirteenth century, when some clever person recognized the potential for using buttons as fasteners. The rest is history.

The designs in this book are based on combining buttons or stacking buttons for the sheer beauty of the buttons--no utilitarian purpose is needed. Over the years buttons have been made from every

trend by wearing jet buttons, a fragile carbon-based material, during mourning for Prince Albert. During Queen Victoria's time jet was expensive and rare, but very much in demand. It was eventually replaced by less expensive and easy to obtain black glass. Buttons have always been a favorite of royalty. Legend has it that King Francis the First of France wore a suit with over 13,000 gold buttons for a meeting with England's Henry VII. Even more over the top, Louis XIV spent $600,000 on buttons in one year! Their passion for buttons makes me feel better about the size of my collection!

As new materials came on the market, new buttons appeared. Shellac was the first "plastic" used for buttons. It was soon replaced by celluloid. Celluloid yellowed and cracked over time and was flammable. Bakelite was discovered while a chemist was looking for an alternative to celluloid to coat wires in electric motors and generators. Bakelite is considered the first true plastic, being made completely from synthetic materials. This was a great choice for buttons, because it was hard and durable.

New buttons are just as beautiful as their vintage cousins and are easily found. JHB has been a leader in bringing beautifully designed buttons to modern crafters. For the designs in this book, experiment with combinations of size, style and color. Remember playing with your mother's button box? That is exactly the way to make your button choices now. First, lay all of your buttons out on a flat surface, then arrange and rearrange them. Try different sizes together, different color combinations, until you find a grouping that grabs you visually. Now you are on your way. The remaining materials are inexpensive and can be found at your local crafts store.

Most of the projects in this book follow a basic recipe. With these three simple ingredients, the possibilities are unlimited.
• The Dazzle: the button, more buttons, stacks of buttons, and a few embellishments like beads, ribbons, and lace.
• The Connector: the means with which you bring everything together whether it's elastic, bead wire, thread, jump rings, or linen cord.
• The Attachment: the way you put it on or the thing you put it on with: pin back, clasp, tee shirt, or sweatshirt.

The most important tool in your toolbox is . . . *your imagination*. It is the one thing that is absolutely required in all of the projects in this book. Your imagination can take an ordinary button and turn it into an extraordinary accessory. Tools required are very simple: scissors to cut thread, ribbon, bead wire, or floss; needles to help string things together; pliers, preferably jeweler's pliers, to bend, shape and connect things. Jeweler's chain nose pliers (our preference) are very versatile and will serve you well in many mediums, because they always have smooth jaws to help keep you from marring your materials.

When I start a project, I pull out all my little embellishments and spend a lot of time relishing in the combination of colors. I add a bit of vintage ribbon here, a little extra bead there, until I come up with a design I like. I love to compare the fashion statements that I can make by combining bits and pieces from my own collection with specialty buttons from the JHB collection. With the high prices at fashion boutiques, I know I come out ahead and with a one-of-a-kind creation.

{ *Button designs on clothing make a fashion boutique statement.* }

Like the creative people at JHB, my love of buttons goes deep. Mrs. Barr loved her buttons so much that she named them. When you visit their site, www.buttons.com, you will run across these endearing names, and by combining our creative forces, I expect you'll fall in love with these projects just the way that I did.

Amy Barickman

P.S. We are introducing a Button Ware line of vintage reproduction buttons! Check our websites for current information.

ban·gle (băng′gəl)

n.

{
1. An ornamental band encircling the wrist
2. An ornament that hangs from a bracelet
}

bracelets & ban

gles

Want to add a little snap to your wardrobe? Elastic plays a role in creating this unique bangle-like bracelet. Stacking chunky buttons will give this project a great dimensional quality.

Stacked Elastic Bracelets

{
Materials

Flat black elastic—appropriate width for buttons of your choosing.

Buttons—number of buttons will depend on size of stacks and circumference of wrist (samples used 1/4" to 3/4"-wide black elastic).

Thread

Optional: Beads for top of stacks
}

Tool Box

Needle

Straight pins

Ruler

Scissors

1 Measure wrist. Cut elastic 2 inches larger than wrist measurement.

2 Determine number of stacks of buttons you want to use. Leaving 1/2-inch at each end of elastic, mark position of stacks evenly spaced on elastic strip with straight pins.

3 Sew button stacks on individually. It is important that each stack is knotted and that the thread is cut between stacks.

4 Overlap the ends of elastic 1/2 inch and sew ends together.

Many of these Bakelite button styles are available in our Button Ware button line from JHB.

Combining long, narrow beads with vertically stacked buttons gives this bracelet added dimension.

Vertical Stacked Elastic Bracelet

Materials
20 inches of 1mm Stretch Magic Jewelry Cord
5 to 6 oblong beads approximately, 1 inch long

5 to 6 stacks of buttons: 5 buttons per stack
Cyanoacrylate glue to seal knot

1 Choose buttons for stacks--try different combination of buttons. The side view of a stack of buttons varies enormously when using various sizes, shapes and colors.

2 Lay out your stacks of buttons and your oblong beads.

3 Take stretchy bead cord and thread on one oblong bead, run your cord along the outside of bead and run thread back through bead in same direction as before (Fig. 1). This will hold your beads in place while stringing.

4 Thread on a stack of beads and an oblong bead. Repeat until the bracelet is the length you want.

5 Go back to first oblong bead and pull cord out of bead, so that cord runs through all beads just once.

6 Thread cord back through all stacks and beads so that cord runs through all beads and buttons twice. Form a circle, pull cord snugly.

7 Tie surgeon's knot (Fig. 2). A surgeon's knot is a square knot with an extra pass over at the end. Add a drop of glue to knot to seal.

Fig. 1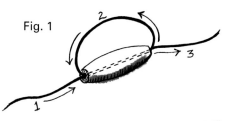

Fig. 2

You can leave out one stack of buttons, and substitute a charm between the remaining two oblong beads

These are quick and easy projects. Because of their simplicity, this project is the perfect way to experiment with the fascinating array of vintage ribbons and trims that are available today.

Ribbon Bracelet

Materials

Buttons—number of buttons will depend on how you choose to embellish your necklace or bracelet.

Ribbon

Necklace end clamps as close to the width of the ribbon as possible.

Extender chain with lobster clasp

Jump rings

Embellishments—beads, ribbon, etc.

Thread

Tool Box

Chain nose jeweler's pliers

Needle

Scissors

Fabri-Tac fabric adhesive

1   Cut ribbon the appropriate length for necklace or bracelet. Fold ends under to the wrong side, 1/4-inch, and secure with Fabri-Tac.

2   After adhesive has dried, apply a small amount of Fabri-Tac to the folded end of ribbon and attach end clamps with pliers.

3   Embellish ribbon with buttons and beads.

4   Attach extender chain and clasp to end clamps with jump rings.

This ribbon bracelet can be adjusted for a necklace as well.

13

This woven, knotted bracelet is a fun and funky addition to any wardrobe. The weaving technique used to connect the buttons can also be done with silk ribbon for a feminine, vintage feel.

Waxed Linen Bracelets

Materials
28 inches of linen, waxed linen, or cotton cord
5 to 8 buttons—the number used will depend on size of button and wrist.

Button clasp or toggle clasp—choice will affect number of buttons.

Tool Box
Cyanoacrylate glue to secure knot

1 Choose button for clasp and set aside (or use toggle clasp). Photos of both styles are shown.

2 Fold cord in half. If using a button for clasp, tie an overhand knot in cord far enough from the end to slip easily over button (Fig. 1). If using toggle clasp, pass one end of cord through the connector loop of the round part of clasp and tie an overhand knot to keep it in place (Fig. 2).

3 Start threading on buttons referring to Fig. 3. Take one cord over the top of button, thread into first button hole and out second buttonhole. Take second cord under button, thread through first hole and out second hole.

4 Tie an overhand knot between each button (Fig.4) or use a bead between buttons by first tying a knot, then threading on a bead and tying another knot.

5 Repeat steps #3 and #4 to end of bracelet.

6 To finish bracelet, thread ends of cord through shank of button reserved for clasp, or toggle part of purchased clasp. Tie an overhand knot (Fig. 5) with ends of cord. Secure with a drop of glue. String a bead or two on the dangling cords and tie a knot to secure beads.

Note: Shanked buttons may be used by tying a knot. Thread a cord through shank and another cord under shank. Pull button close to knot. Tie another knot close to shank. Continue with next button. For a modern look, use a 1mm leather cord.

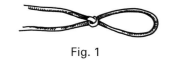

Fig. 1

Fig. 2

Fig. 3

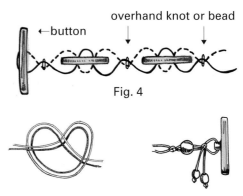

Fig. 4

overhand knot   Fig. 5

{ *Try creating a necklace using this waxed linen technique.* }

15

Take full advantage of your button stash with this delightfully easy project. If your collection doesn't include plenty of shanked buttons, you can use plastic button shanks to convert them.

Shanked Button Elastic Bracelets

Materials

Assortment of shanked buttons—
the number will depend on size of buttons.
Beads—numbers will depend on size of beads
and length of bracelet.
20 inches of Stretch Magic Jewelry Cord
Clear plastic button shank findings if needed.

Tool Box

Scissors
Cyanoacrylate glue
E6000 adhesive

1 Measure wrist. Add one inch. Lay out buttons. Experiment with positions to fit wrist measurement. Measure space between buttons from shank to shank.

2 Thread on first button; then thread on enough beads to reach next button measurement.

3 Repeat until you have all buttons threaded on and finish with a group of beads.

4 At this point thread cord through buttons and beads again (starting with first button) for extra strength.

5 Tie an overhand knot (Fig.1). Apply a drab of glue to knot. Trim and pull knot through beads so it is hidden.

Note: Use clear plastic button shank findings to convert non-shank buttons. Use E6000 adhesive to adhere shanks to buttons.

Fig. 1

This simple-to-create bracelet can run the gamut from elegant to whimsical,
depending on your choice of buttons.

Button Disk-Loop Bracelets

{
Materials
Purchased disc-loop bracelet blank
Buttons—the number of buttons required will
depend on the size of your buttons and the
number of buttons per stack.
Seed beads

Thread

Tool Box
Needle
E6000 adhesive
}

1 Glue buttons that will be stacked together, making
sure button holes are clear of glue.

2 After glue has dried, add seed beads to button
centers by sewing them on with thread.

3 Glue buttons to discs. You can either glue one
button per disk or for larger buttons, glue one
button to two disks. (Fig. 1)

←button

bracelet →

Fig. 1

{
*There are as many
alternatives for
stacking buttons as
there are styles of
buttons. Experiment
with different
arrangements.*
}

Delicate and graceful, this bracelet is truly "charming."
The project uses buttons instead of traditional charms.

Charmingly Graceful

{

Materials
Chain bracelet with clasp
Buttons—the number will depend on what you choose to use on your bracelet.
Charms—the number will depend on what you want your bracelet to look like.
Beads
Head pins—3" long
Jump rings
20 gauge wire

Tool Box
Chain nose jeweler's pliers
Wire cutter

}

1 Arrange buttons and charms in a manner that pleases you.

2 To make charms from buttons, take a 6-inch piece of wire and fold it in half. Thread button on wire (Fig.1). While holding the wire tightly against the button, use pliers to form a loop in one end of the wire. Slip the wire through the link in the chain in desired position. Wrap the opposite wire tightly around the first wire to form a loop. Trim any excess wire.

3 You can add a dangle to the button by taking a head pin and threading on a bead. Run the head pin through the second buttonhole (Fig. 2). Fold head pin in over the sides of the button, so that bead is about 1/4-inch from bottom of the button. Wrap the head pin wire tightly around itself (Fig.3). Trim the excess wire.

4 Add charms with jump rings by spreading ring, then slipping on a charm. Slip onto chain link and close the jump ring.

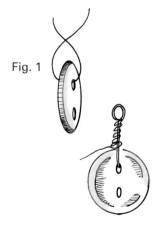

Fig. 1

Fig. 2

← bead
← headpin

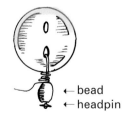

Fig. 3

← bead
← headpin

Buttons give this lively charm bracelet movement and rhythm.
It looks elaborate, but looks are deceiving, because it's a snap to assemble.

Charmingly Simple

{
Materials
Chain bracelet with clasp
Buttons—1 or 2 buttons with shank for each
link of chain.
Jump rings—1 for every button

Tool Box
Chain nose jeweler's pliers
}

1 Experiment with different layouts of buttons.
You should have one button for each chain link.

Fig. 1a

2 Take bracelet, at one end, begin attaching buttons.
Spread jump ring with pliers, slip on shanked
button, attach to chain link and close jump ring.

3 Continue alternating sides of chain links as you
attach buttons (Fig.1a) or button on each side of
each link (Fig. 1b).

Fig. 1b

A diverse array of buttons gives this bracelet texture and substance. Your choice of color defines the mood.

This is a stunning button bracelet, that will almost certainly bead-dazzle you. A double strand of beads adds extra sparkle. This project gives you a chance to show off your best buttons.

Stacked Beaded Bracelets

Materials
26 inches .019 (.4mm) bead wire
1 crimp bead
Beads—8/0 or 6/0 are good
Buttons—the number will depend on size of buttons and number of buttons per stack.
1 small stop button
1 closing button (or stack of buttons for closing)
Optional: Ribbon
            Thread

Tool Box
Crimp tool
Measuring chart
Mechanical pencil
Needle

1 Choose your buttons--experiment with color and size combinations. Stacking buttons will provide good color, texture, and depth and also will make your bracelet more interesting. Measure your wrist and cut a length of paper the same length as the wrist measurement. This is your measuring chart.

2 Take bead wire and string enough beads to pass comfortably around the closing button. Pull beads to the center of the bead wire. Thread on stop bead, one bead thread through each hole in button to form a loop (Fig. 1).

3 Use measuring chart to plan button positions. Hold bead loop at one end of chart and mark where stop bead falls. Position buttons evenly in the remaining space, marking holes in buttons on chart with pencil.

4 String an equal number of beads on each bead wire to reach first mark on chart. Thread both bead wires through one bead. Thread one bead wire through the stack of buttons, put a bead on wire and pass wire back through the top of the button stack. On back of button stack, take the remaining bead wire and string two beads. Thread bead wire from the button stack through the last bead of the other bead wire (Fig. 2). Gently pull to tighten. This should form a lock at the back of the beads with both bead wires. Continue in this manner, using measuring chart as you go.

5 After the last button stack has been locked, thread 3 beads on each bead wire, then thread both bead wires through one bead and the crimp bead. Thread both bead wires through the first hole of the closing button, add a bead, bring wires through second hole in button and back through the crimp bead and next bead (Fig. 3). Gently pull to tighten and use the crimp tool to close crimp bead. Thread bead wires separately through a few beads to hide and carefully clip bead wire.

6 For an extra feminine detail, tie a pretty ribbon around the bracelet next to the closing loop. Tack with thread to secure.

Chunkier stacks give this bracelet more dimension.

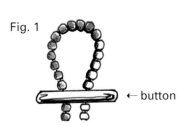

Fig. 1

← button

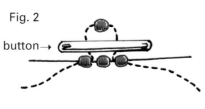

Fig. 2

button →

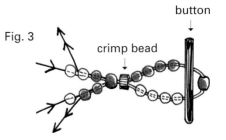

button

Fig. 3

crimp bead

25

Using mother-of pearl-buttons, beads, silk ribbons, and more—this combination makes for a stunning fabric cuff. You can sew it by hand or on a machine.

Fabric Cuff Bracelet

Materials

1 piece of 6-1/2" x 5" fabric –torn, not cut

2 pieces of 3-1/2" x 1" fabric –cut

3 pieces of braid trim, 6-1/2" long, 1/2" to 3/4" wide

2/3 yard of 1/2" wide silk ribbon

Buttons—1 large, 1" diameter, for clasp,

and an assortment to use for embellishing.

Beads—assorted

Thread

Tool Box

Scissors

Needle

Iron

Optional: Sewing machine

1 Tear a 6-1/2" x 5" piece of fabric. Fold fabric in half so that you have a 6-1/2" x 2-1/2" piece. Press flat. Fray long edges.

2 With right sides together, place the 3-1/2" x 1" fabric piece onto one end of folded fabric cuff, aligning raw edges, leaving 1/2" at top and bottom (Fig.1a and 1b). Sew together using a 1/4" seam allowance. Repeat on opposite end. Press flat.

3 By hand or machine, sew braid trim onto the outside of the cuff.

4 Fold length over 1/4 inch. Fold over again 3/8 inch, encasing ends of braided trim, then press. Stitch down (Fig. 2).

5 On right side, sew clasp button on one end of cuff. Embellish with buttons and beads.

6 At opposite end of cuff, tie a bow in silk ribbon at one end, leaving a 2-inch tail, stitch through center of bow to hold. Tie another bow at other end of ribbon, leaving a 4-inch gap between the centers of bows. Stitch through the center of bow to hold.

7 Sew bows on corners of the other end of the cuff to form a loop for the clasp button (Fig. 3).

Fig. 1a

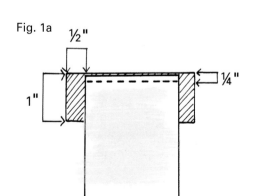

Fig. 1b

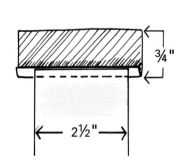

Fig. 2

Fig. 3

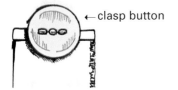

← clasp button

{ *Using a double silk ribbon bow makes this cuff unique. The possibilities are endless when it comes to using vintage or contemporary trim.* }

pen·dant (pĕn´dənt)

n.

{ 1. An ornament (as on a
    necklace) allowed to
    hang free }

necklaces, chok

ers & pendants

Never underestimate the romance of a simple mother-of-pearl button. This charming choker brings out the most flattering qualities of these sweet buttons.

Mother-of-Pearl Wire Choker

{
Materials
Buttons
20 gauge wire
Pre-made choker-ribbon: leather, linen, rubber
Optional: Bead or shanked button for dangle

Tool Box
Chain nose jeweler's pliers
Wire cutters
}

1   For a single button or a single stack pendant, cut 6 inches of wire and fold wire in half. Thread the button (or stack) on to the wire. Thread each wire into remaining hole. The wire will come out of opposite side of the button (Fig.1).

2   Pull wires snugly to the top of the button. Form a loop with one wire, making sure that the loop is big enough to fit over the clasp of the choker.

3   Wrap the other wire snugly around the first wire, trim with the wire cutters (Fig. 2).

4   Thread onto the choker.

Note: For the dangle, during Step 1, thread the shanked button or the bead on to the wire before threading the main button onto the wire (Fig. 3).

Fig. 1

Fig. 2

Fig. 3

← dangle button

{ *You can use a purchased choker or make your own. Try colored buttons for a* }

Funky, chunky pendants are an easy way to use sassy, colorful buttons to brighten your wardrobe. This is the simple, basic recipe for stacked pendants.

Basic Stacked Pendants

Materials
2mm leather cord (or ribbon)
Choker end caps
Chain and clasp with jump rings (or pre-made choker).
1 stack of buttons—the number of buttons will depend on what you want your stack to look like.
Clothing clasp or suitably sized flat-backed charm for pendant bail.

Jump rings

Tool Box
Chain nose jeweler's pliers
E6000 adhesive

1 Glue button stack together.

2 Glue one-half of the clothing clasp or charm pendant to the back of stack.

3 Thread onto the leather cord. Put dab of glue on cord ends and attach end caps. Finish by adding chain and clasp to the end caps with jump rings.

Note: You can thread stacked pendant onto ribbon and tie at neck. Also, note in the photo on page 33 that the classic JHB clasp was converted into a pendant bail.

Simple and stylish
—the chunkier
the stack, the
more interesting
the pendant.

For earthy romance, try using all natural materials to create this striking pendant using the best autumn colors that Mother Nature has to offer.

Nature's Touch Pendant

Materials

At least 30 buttons ranging in size from 1/2" to 1-1/4" in diameter. Buttons are all natural wood or horn (or man made look-alikes) and buttons with antique silver finish.
1 shank button for clasp (optional)
1 "E" seed bead, 6/0 size, or other bead of similar size (approximately 1/8").
1 flat wooden bead, 1/4"
1 round wood bead, 1/8"

8 rondel (flattened round) wood or 1/4" metal spacer beads.
1 package (containing at least 4 feet) of 1 mm leather cord.
Scrap of wire approximately 6" long (a long twist tie will also work).

Tool Box

Chain nose jeweler's pliers
Scissors

1   Bend one end of the scrap of wire into a loop. Thread buttons on the scrap of wire to "preview" how they will look in the final project. Using the wire scrap makes it quick and easy to try many combinations. In this project it is the profile or side of the button and how the buttons nest together that counts, not the face of the button. So, sometimes you will want buttons threaded back-to-back or face-to-face, rather than with the face of the buttons all in the same direction. Keep playing with the arrangement until you are satisfied with color and profile.

2   When satisfied with the arrangement of the buttons, thread the seed bead onto the middle of a 4- foot length of leather cord. Beginning with the bottom-most button, transfer the buttons from the wire scrap to one end of the beading thread.

3   Pick up the remaining end of the leather cord and thread through the stack of buttons. On buttons with four holes, thread the cord through the hole opposite the first cord.

4   Thread both cords through the flat wooden bead and the small round wood bead. Knot the cord at the top of the pendant. If the leather cord is snug in the top bead, a knot may be unnecessary.

5   Tie an overhand knot in each end of the cord approximately 2" above the pendant. Thread on a rondel bead, five small buttons and another rondel bead. Knot again close to the bead.

6   Knot each end again approximately 5" from the last knot. Thread on a rondel bead, three slightly larger buttons, and a rondel bead and knot.

7   Tie the ends of the cord at the desired length with a square knot. Or, alternatively, tie a shank button on one end of the cord. On the remaining end, tie a loop large enough to slip over the button to complete the clasp.

These colorful beads make a trendy, modern statement that is sure to attract attention.

Bright and Sassy Pendant

Materials

At least 13 buttons, ranging in size from 1/4" to 1-3/8" diameter. These Buttons are bright pastels in pink, turquoise and green with several novelty buttons.

1 small flat bead, approximately 1/4" in diameter

1 crystal bead, a scant 1/8" in diameter

1 crystal bead, a generous 1/8" in diameter

1 diamond-shaped crystal bead, approximately 1/4" long

1 package of size 6/0 "E" size seed beads

Heavy nylon beading thread

Heavy duty magnetic catch

Scrap of wire, approximately 6" long (a long twist tie will also work).

Tool Box

Craft or cyanoacrylate glue

Chain nose jeweler's pliers

Scissors

1 Decide on the button order as in step 1 of Nature's Touch Pendant.

2 When satisfied with the arrangement of the buttons, thread the smaller crystal bead onto the middle of a 4-foot length of nylon beading thread. Thread both ends of the thread through the flat bead. Beginning with the bottom-most button, transfer the buttons from the wire scrap to one end of the beading thread.

3 Pick up the remaining thread end and thread through the stack of buttons. On buttons with four holes, thread the cord through the hole opposite the first cord.

4 Pass both threads through the smaller remaining crystal bead, then through the larger diamond-shaped crystal bead.

5 Separate the thread ends, and on each, thread on seed beads to the desired length.

6 Tie each thread end onto one section of the magnetic catch. Put a drop of glue on the knot to secure. When dry, thread ends back through a few seed beads and trim.

Keeping with the themes of nature these leafy green beads, highlighted with shades of reds and yellows, add a Tuscany flavor to your wardrobe.

Vineyard Pendant

Materials

At least 15 buttons ranging in size from 3/8" to 1-3/8" in diameter. Buttons are vineyard colors--grape, leaf green, rich red, orange and ginger.

1 round textured bead

1 rondel (flattened round) glass or wood bead

3 beads with large holes (optional)

1 foot-length of color-coordinated 20-gauge craft wire

4 feet of color coordinated rattail rayon cord

Scrap of wire approximately 6" long (a long twist tie will do).

Tool Box

Round nose jeweler's pliers

Chain nose jeweler's pliers

Craft or cyanoacrylate glue

1 Decide on the button order as in step 1 of Nature's Touch Pendant.

2 When satisfied with the arrangement of the buttons, fold the length of craft wire in half into a U shape. Beginning with the bottom-most button, transfer the buttons from the wire scrap onto the craft wire. On buttons with four holes, make sure that the wire is threaded through opposite holes of the button. Thread both wires through the 1/2" bead, and the rondel bead.

3 Snug the buttons and beads closely together on the wire. Treating both wires as one, grasp the wire with needle nose pliers and bend wire down against jaws of pliers making a right angle bend a scant 1/4" above the last bead (Fig. 1). Using the round nose pliers, roll the pliers toward the bend, forming a circle (Fig. 2). With the needle nose pliers, grasp where the wires cross and tightly wind the wire ends around the base of the loop. Continue wrapping until the wraps meet the top bead (Fig. 3). Unroll a half turn, trim wire ends and rewrap. (For more detailed instructions and photos of process, search for "wrapped wire loop" on the Internet.)

4 Thread the rattail cord through the wire loop. Tie in a square knot at the desired length. For a more finished cord, thread the three beads onto one end of the cord. From the opposite direction, thread the remaining cord end through the three beads (Fig. 4). Adjust cord length. Use craft glue to secure beads and trim off the excess cord length.

Fig. 1

¼"

Fig. 2

Fig. 3

Fig. 4

Necklaces, Chokers & Pendants

The clever use of stacked green buttons gives this project plenty of holiday cheer. Play with imaginative ribbon to add a touch of whimsy.

Christmas Tree Necklace

Materials

1 purchased cord necklace

1 shanked button for tree base

5 green buttons of graduated sizes

4 green 4mm beads

1 red crystal bead, 8 mm, for top of tree

1 necklace end clamp set (including end chain and clasp)

24 gauge wire

Thread

Tool Box

Chain nose jeweler's pliers

Fabri-Tac fabric glue

Wire cutters

Needle

1   Cut 12 inches of wire and fold the wire in half. Thread shanked button to the middle of the wire.

2   Thread the largest button on the wire. Run wires through separate holes (Fig. 1). Bring both wires together. Pull tight and twist twice.

3   Thread both wires through a bead.

4   Thread the next size button on the wire, running both wires through one hole (Fig. 2). This will give the tree a bit of whimsical movement.

5   Repeat steps 3 and 4.

6   Thread red bead on both wires.

7   Twist wires together. Form a loop (for cord and clasp to run through). Grasp loop with pliers and wrap wire tail around stem between bead and loop (Fig. 3). Trim excess wrapping wire with wire cutters.

8   Thread the tree onto the cord necklace.

Fig. 1

Fig. 2

Fig. 3

This clever project can be used to adorn your neck— or your home. When it comes to holiday pendants, think about gift-giving and tree-trimming.

41

Charming beads and a bit of crochet, add a graceful twist to this button necklace.
The technique beautifully showcases larger, standout pieces from your button collection.

Crocheted Beaded Button Pendant

{

Materials

8 feet of 1mm linen or cotton cord

7 to 9 buttons, 2-hole, with the following sizes: 3 buttons, 1/2" or 3/8"; 1 large button; 1 medium; and the remaining buttons will be stacked.

E or 6mm Beads with hole large enough for 1mm cord to pass through easily.

Tool Box

Size 2 steel crochet hook

Scissors

}

1 Arrange buttons in three stacks:
Stack A--medium-sized button stack
Stack B--3 buttons, 1/2" or 3/8" size
Stack C--large button stack
Reserve one or two buttons for clasp.

2 Fold cord in half. Thread Stack A on by threading one end of the cord into first hole, under and into the second hole. Take the other end of the cord, and going in the opposite direction, thread into first hole, over and into second hole (Fig.1). Pull cords tight. Make an overhand knot (Fig. 2).

3 Thread on Stack B (three small buttons), running one cord through each hole (Fig. 3). Pull tight. Make an overhand knot.

4 Repeat step 3 with Stack C.

5 Make a slip knot next to the overhand knot with one half of the cord. Use this to start a single crochet chain. Thread beads one at a time, and crochet into chain at even intervals, approximately 1" apart. Crochet until you are four inches from end of the cord. Tie off.

6 Thread clasp button stack on. Tie an overhand knot snugly against crocheted chain (Fig. 4).

7 Repeat with the other cord, but this time chain stitch to one inch from end of cord. Fold chain cord over to form loop big enough to slip over the clasp button. Single crochet into chain and tie off (Fig.5).

Note: For more detailed crochet instructions search the internet for "Basic Crochet Instructions."

Fig. 1   Fig. 2   Fig. 3   Fig. 4   Fig. 5

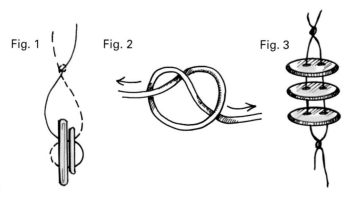

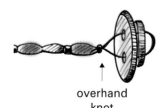

overhand knot

{ *Using a stack of buttons and a cord loop is a great way to make your own closures.* }

*This fun pattern can use either your own button stash or select a variety from the store. Either way,
you are sure to make a one-of-a-kind piece of art with this pattern.*

Button Collage Necklaces

Materials
Pleather 1mm Cording: 3 meter package
Buttons, minimum of 30 small to large sizes
2-holed, 4-holed, and shank.
2 sterling silver cones, small or medium-sized.
2 small sterling silver beads, 2-3mm to fit over small
end of cone.
1 sterling silver split ring, 5 mm
1 sterling silver split ring, 7mm
1 sterling silver lobster claw clasp
1 wire, 12" long, 22-gauge, half hard,
sterling silver.

Tool Box
Wire cutters
Chain nose jeweler's pliers
Round nose jeweler's pliers
Scissors
Gem Tac white glue
Beading mat
Tape measure or ruler

1 Lay out your buttons by color, then size and style on the bead mat in front of you.

2 Cut the three meters of Pleather into three, 1-meter sections. Lay them out in front of you. Choose a larger or somewhat unique button for your centerpiece. Slide that onto the center of one of your cords.

3 Add buttons on to the other cords. Keep some space with some cording showing between the buttons so they show off well. It is best to use two cords together frequently. This ties the cords together and makes it appear as if it is all one piece instead of having one cord hanging off all alone (Fig. 1).

4 Watch so your colors and sizes are mixed well throughout the whole piece. It helps to lay out the buttons in a loose order in front of you making sure you get colors and styles spaced well. Be flexible, though, as you may change your mind as the piece starts to evolve.

5 Buttons will be visible from both sides. If a button has a back that you would prefer not to show, be sure to stack it back-to-back with another button. Stacking buttons on top of each other, up to three buttons, is a great way to get height and unique texture (Fig. 2).

continued on page 46

Fig. 1

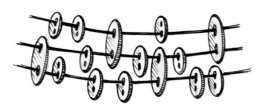

Fig. 2

*Choose many brightly colored
buttons or choose a monochromatic
theme for a dramatically
different look.*

Shank: Slide it on one cord. It must have a stationary button on each side to keep it in place. You can have the two stationary buttons separated by an inch or so, but know that the shank button will move as you wear it. Or you can have the stationary buttons tight against the shank button so it has little or no movement. Remember you will see the shank button from the back as well, so take this into consideration.

Two-Holed Buttons: The easiest ones to use in stacks.

Slider: String the cord through one hole from the back to the front and slide the button in place. Thread the cord through the other hole from front to back. If the holes in the button are tight on the cord, then the button will stay in place and can be used as a stationary button. If the holes in the button are large, then the button may slide a bit giving some movement.

Connector: String one cord through a hole on the button and string another cord through the other hole. This is a great way to bring cords together and allow cord gatherings. This may also allow buttons to slide, depending on the hole sizes and space allowed.

Four-Holed Buttons: The easiest ones to use alone.

Stationary: String the cord through one hole from the back to the front. Position the button. Bring the cord

down a hole next to the first one, threading from the front to the back. Bring the cord diagonally across the back to that hole and thread to the front again. Lastly, bring the cord to the back again through the one remaining hole. This button should now hold tight.

Connector: String one cord from the back to the front in any hole. Move diagonally across the front and string the cord from the front to the back. Now take another cord and string the cord into the open hole closest to your cord from the front to the back and cross over the back diagonally. Go through the one remaining hole from the back to the front. Pull tight.

Another Connector: The same as above but cross both cords over each other in the front.

Finishing Off

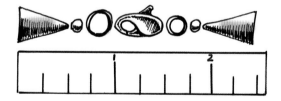

Continue adding buttons to within about six inches from the end of each cord. Now is the time to figure out how long to make the finished piece. Lay the following supplies out next to a tape measure or ruler: a cone, a bead, the smaller split ring, the lobster claw, the smaller split ring, a bead and a cone. Figure the full length of all these pieces. Take the desired completed length of your piece, subtract the finding's length and mark the cords with the remaining length. Leave at least an inch of cord uncovered from the buttons to the cones. Now is the time to add more buttons.

Wrapped Loops

1 Cut the foot of wire in half. Grab one of the wires with the chain nose pliers 2" from the end. Using your thumb tight against the pliers, bend the wire with your thumb over the pliers to form a tight right angle in your wire.

2 With the round nose in an up-and-down position, grab the 2" piece tight in the corner and bend the wire up and over the pliers to form a half-circle.

3 Reposition the round nose pliers with the bottom jaw into the half-circle and the top jaw holding onto the top of the wire circle.

4 Bend the wire under the pliers to form the rest to the circle. Make sure this circle is large enough to fit all three cords through it.

5 Move the round nose pliers, still gripping the circle, to your less dominant hand. Holding the circle for leverage in this hand, pick up the chain nose pliers and grab the very tip of the tail of the 2" piece of wire and wrap it tightly around the 4" piece.

Wrap twice with one wrap tight up against the circle to close and tighten the circle and the other wrap down the shaft of the wire. Cut off excess and tuck excess wire in.

6 Slide the three cords from one side of the necklace through the wire circle. Tie a tight overhand knot using all of the cords over the bottom of the wire circle.

7 Take the chain nose pliers and squeeze your wire circle into an up-and-down tight oval, to fit in the cone better. Pull the wire with the cords into the cone, checking to make sure everything fits.

8 Remove the wire, put a layer of glue around the knot, and pull it tight up into cone with a good yank. Cut off the excess leather when the glue has dried.

9 String the bead on the wire above the cone. Grab the wire with the chain nose pliers tight against the bead and about a 1/4" or less in on the plier's jaws. Using your thumb against the pliers, form a tight right angle.

Following steps 1 to 6 for a wrapped loop, complete a wrapped loop above the cone and bead. Stop your wraps a half of a turn before the ends, cut, then tuck the wire into the end.

Slide the smaller split ring on the loop and attach the lobster claw clasp (or any type clasp would work) to the split ring. Finish the other side in the same way.

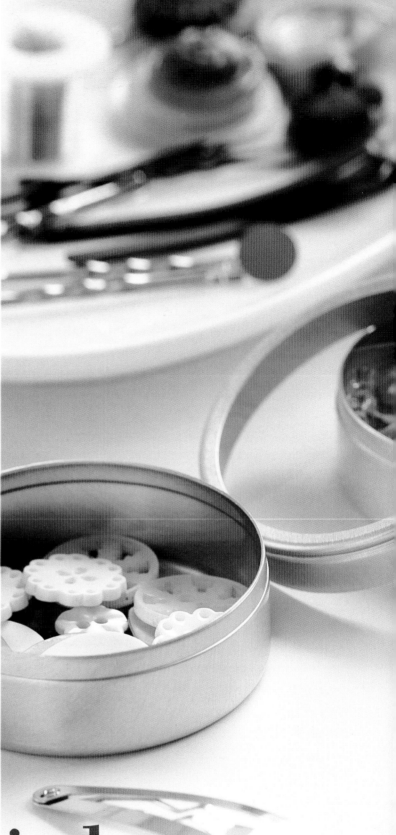

a·dorn (ə-dôrn´)

vt.

{
1. To enhance the beauty
2. To decorate
}

embellishments

& adornments

Colorful beadwork frames beautiful buttons in this fun project.

Beaded Button Pins

{

Materials
Buttons—the number of buttons will depend on your personal preference and the size of the buttons. Wool felt for backing, at least an 8-inch square. Beads—E or 6 mm and other assorted styles for embellishment.
Thread
Pin back

Tool Box
4-inch embroidery hoop
Needle
E6000 adhesive

}

1 Secure the felt in embroidery hoop. Glue button to felt. If you are stacking buttons, glue the largest button to felt. After glue dries, sew the rest of the stack to felt-backed button, adding a bead to the top of the button stack.

2 Thread the needle, double, and knot.

3 Run needle from back of felt next to button's edge. String enough beads on thread to circle button snugly. Run needle through felt to back of work (Fig.1).

4 Bring needle up through felt, next to the button, 2-3 beads distance from the original position. Run needle over bead thread to couch (Fig. 2).

5 Repeat couching all around the button. Knot the thread and cut.

6 Cut the button out of the felt, trimming very close to edge of beads. Be careful to avoid accidentally cutting the bead thread.

7 Lay the button on a piece of excess felt and cut a circle of felt the same size as the beaded button. Whipstitch felt circle to the button.

8 Sew a beaded picot trim to the edge (Fig. 3).

9 Sew on pin back.

Fig. 1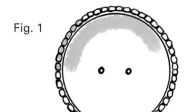

Fig. 2

Fig. 3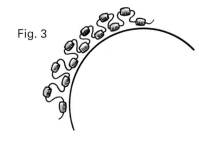

Embellishments & Adornments

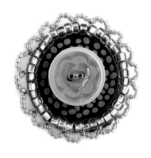

A ring of beads surrounding a stack of buttons creates a frame for your favorite "work of art."

Pretty posies created from buttons make a sunny fashion statement. Wire-wrapping techniques finish off this clever brooch, giving it more dimension.

Button Bouquet Pins

{
Materials
3 to 10 buttons—the number will depend on how many flowers you decide to make and if you stack the buttons.

20 gauge wire: Either floral stem wire (covered or plain) or 18-inch lengths of craft wire, one length for each flower, plus one additional length to wrap bouquet.

Ribbon

Pin back

Optional: Beads for center of flowers (with holes large enough for wire to pass through).

Tool Box
Chain nose jeweler's pliers

Wire cutters

E6000 adhesive
}

1 Choose an odd number of buttons (3 to 5) to represent flower heads. If you are stacking buttons, arrange into stacks.

2 Fold all but one 18-inch length wire in half.

3 From bottom of button, thread the wire through one hole of button or stack. If desired, first thread on beads for center of flower. Place button assembly in center of wire and thread wire down through the other hole. Pull snug and twist the wire to form stem and leaves (Fig.1).

4 Repeat step 3 for each flower.

5 Gather flowers, adjusting stem lengths and lightly twist together. Glue pin back to stem.

6 Open pin back and using the remaining piece of wire, tightly wrap the flower bundle (Fig. 2). Trim the ends. Tuck the ends into bundle.

7 Tie with ribbon. Curl ends of stems (Fig 3).

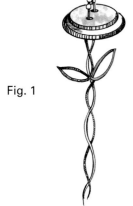

Fig. 1

Fig. 2

Fig. 3

{ *A few buttons, a little wire, and a bit of ribbon are transformed into a sweet statement. Experiment with different ways of twisting the wires.* }

Funky, fun, fabric swatches give these simple statements the flower power you need to jazz up any outfit.

Fabric Flower Pins

Materials
2 3/4" x 9" strip of fabric
Buttons for center of flower
Beads
Silk leaves
Pin back
Thread

Tool Box
Needle
Iron
Optional: E6000 adhesive

1 Tear a 2 3/4" x 9" strip of fabric. Fray edges.

2 With wrong sides together, fold fabric in half on the lengthwise, 1-1/2" from long edge (Fig.1). Press the fold with an iron.

3 Unfold the fabric strip, lengthwise. With right sides together, sew short ends using a 1/4" seam allowance, to form a tube. Refold along the pressed line.

4 Sew a basting seam along the folded edge. Gather to form a flower. Knot securely.

5 Sew or glue a button or a stack of buttons to the center of fabric, adding beads to top if desired.

6 Glue or sew one or two silk leaves to the back of flower.

7 Glue or sew a pin back to the back of flower.

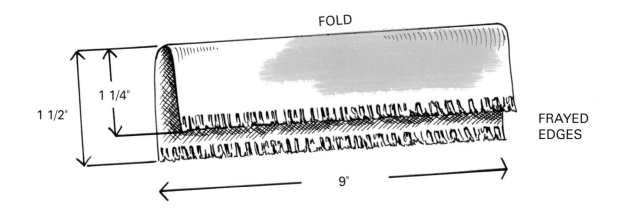

FOLD

1 1/4"

1 1/2"

9"

FRAYED EDGES

{ *If you want a more contemporary look, try leaving off the silk leaves.* }

Rectangles, squares—modern or vintage—the designs and uses of these button pins are only limited by your imagination.

Stacked Button Pins

Materials

Buttons—the number and size of buttons will depend on your creative vision.

Beads for top embellishment

28 gauge wire or thread

Pin back

Optional: Large bead or several small beads for the top of stack.

Tool Box

Chain nose jeweler's pliers

Wire cutters

E6000 adhesive or Devcon 2-part Epoxy

1 Choose buttons of graduated sizes, experimenting with size and color. Try different buttons or beads to top off stack.

2 Stack buttons, line up button holes, and secure with a small amount of adhesive, making sure holes are clear of glue. Thread wire or thread through the holes. Knot the thread or twist the wire on the back side of button stack to secure. If you are using wire, clip it close to the button and run back up into closest buttonhole.

3 Glue on pin back.

Embellishments & Adornments

A sprinkling of these delightful accessories will add a new dimension to your hair and take full advantage of your button collection. This requires a minimum investment, but it pays stylish dividends.

Bobbys & Barrettes

{
Materials
Buttons
Bobby pins or hair clips
Thread
Optional: Beads

Tool Box
Devcon 2-Part Epoxy or E6000 adhesive
Needle
}

1 Use thread to tie button stacks together. Use a few little beads to top off buttons (Fig.1). Little pearls or crystals are good choices.

2 Mix 2-Part Epoxy, dip rounded end of bobby pin in epoxy and glue to back of button stack with crimped part of bobby pin against button (Fig. 2).

Note: If using hair clips, follow step 1, then glue button stack to the flat end of hair clip.

Fig. 1

Fig. 2

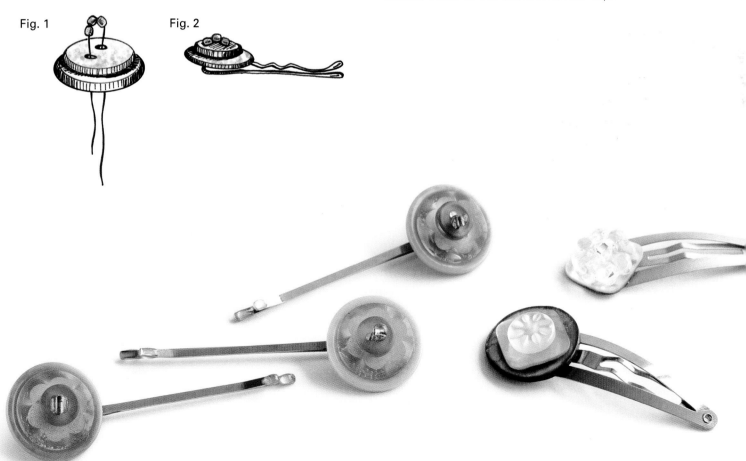

A few well-chosen buttons make these distinctive rings special. These are quick and easy to make.
Picking out your buttons is the hardest part.

Elastic Button Rings

Materials
1/2"-wide black braided elastic
3 Buttons—1 large 2-holed or 4-holed
1 medium 2-holed or 4-holed
1 rounded top, shank or flat back
Black thread

Tool Box
Needle
Scissors
Wire cutters
E6000 adhesive

1 Measure around your ring finger, plus 1/2," to determine the length of the elastic. Cut elastic.

2 Measure 1/4" from the end of the elastic and fold back, wrong sides together (Fig. 1). Overlap 1/4" to opposite end of elastic and stitch to form a ring. Make sure the ring fits comfortably before sewing on buttons. Knot securely.

3 Sew large button to elastic on the outside of the ring, over the stitch line.

4 Sew the medium button on top of large button. Knot securely.

5 If necessary, cut the shank off the remaining button. Glue button on the top of the button stack.

Fig. 1   1/4 "

Embellishments & Adornments

Wire loops add earthy element to stylish statements.

Wire Button Rings

{ Materials
Stack of buttons
Bead for center of buttons
18 inches of 20 gauge wire

Tool Box
Ring mandrel
Chain nose jeweler's pliers
Wire cutters }

1 Measure for ring size with a piece of scrap wire.

2 Start the ring on mandrel, 2 sizes bigger than the ring size you decided on.

3 Hold the wire to mandrel 10 inches from the end of wire. Start to wrap both ends of wire around the mandrel in opposite directions. Wrap 2-3 times.

4 Bring both ends of the wire together. Run the longer wire up through button stack hole, through bead, and back down through the other hole (Fig.1). Wrap this wire around the mandrel one more time.

5 Wrap the remaining wires around each side of the ring (Fig. 2). Trim the wire and push flush with pliers.

Fig. 1

Fig. 2

fash·ion (făsh´ən)

n.

{
1. Current style
2. To make or form something
}

fashion apparel

Recycled wool men's sweater and salvaged buttons make a fun and funky addition to any wardrobe. Think green!

Recycled Heart Sweater

Materials

1 recycled men's wool sweater

1 7" x7" square of red fleece

1 3" x3" square of fleece in a different red with different texture.

36 to 40 white buttons in various sizes—use salvaged buttons cut from clothes you are discarding.

White embroidery floss

2 yards ball fringe

Contrasting thread to sew on buttons

Tool Box

Fabri-Tac fabric adhesive

Sewing machine

Scissors

Needle

Pins

1 Determine the length you want the sweater to be. Mark with pins. Sew a line of zigzag stitches with sewing machine around the pin line. Cut off the bottom of the sweater.

2 With zigzag stitches, sew ball fringe to the bottom of sweater.

3 Hand sew a 7" x7" square of red fleece to the front of the sweater with white embroidery floss. Use a decorative stitch of your choice.

4 Cut a heart out of the second piece of fleece and sew to center of a 7" x7" square with white embroidery floss. Use decorative stitch of your choice. Refer to photograph for ideas.

5 Sew buttons randomly on background square with contrasting thread.

This hip and sophisticated tee shirt will get noticed! It looks like a designer exclusive, but looks are deceiving and surprisingly affordable.

Button Spray Tee

{
Materials

Tee shirt

15 multi-colored buttons--5/8" and 3/4"

21 mother-of-pearl buttons--1/2" and 3/4"

36 black beads

Black thread

Tool Box

Fabri-Tac fabric adhesive

Needle
}

1 Lay tee shirt flat. Referring to the photograph, lay out buttons in design shown. Use a small amount of Fabri-Tac to secure the buttons to tee. Keep the button holes clear of glue.

2 Sew buttons to tee. Add a bead to the center of each button. Knot and clip thread between buttons.

Add originality to a shirt or tee in the color of your choice. Varying the size of buttons adds interest to the small cross. Also consider creating this design with a series of heirloom mother-of-pearl buttons— no need for exact matches—the more unique the better!

Contemporary Cross

{

Materials
Solid color tee or tank shirt
9 buttons, 3/8" mother-of-pearl
10 buttons, 1/2" mother-of-pearl
8 buttons, 5/8" mother-of-pearl
Thread to match your tee shirt or buttons

Tool Box
Fabri-Tac fabric adhesive
Needle

}

1 Arrange the cross on your shirt referring to the photograph.

2 Stabilize the cross design by using a small amount of fabric glue on the back of each button. Keep the button holes clear of glue.

3 Stitch the buttons in place using a thread color that coordinates with either the shirt or button.

Embellish your favorite solid colored shirt with buttons in the shape of a heart and make it a real conversational clothing item!

Conversational Heart Tee

Materials
Solid color tee shirt
25 assorted silver or pewter buttons, minimum
Thread to coordinate with tee shirt or buttons

Tool Box
Paper
Scissors
Pins
Needle
Fabri-Tac fabric adhesive

1 Using the heart pattern shown, trace and cut out a paper heart for pattern. Try shirt on for correct placement and pin the pattern to the shirt.

2 Lay the shirt flat. Place buttons around the paper heart, varying shape, texture and size. Use both the right and wrong side of the buttons for additional texture and shape.

3 Stabilize your heart button design by using a small amount of fabric glue on the back of each button. Keep the button holes clear of glue.

4 Stitch buttons in place using a thread color that coordinates with either the shirt or the buttons.

Bright buttons form the centerpiece of this lively, abstract design.

Rickrack Abstract Sweatshirt

Materials

1 child's sweatshirt

1 4"x 8" piece complementary color sweatshirt material.

26" piece jumbo rickrack

1 yard ball fringe

7 buttons in assorted colors and sizes: three in 1-3/8" diameter; three in 1" diameter; one in 5/8" diameter.

3 colors embroidery thread

Sewing thread to match rickrack

Tool Box

Needle

Scissors

Optional: Sewing machine

1 Cut the waistband from the sweatshirt.

2 Hand or machine stitch a rectangle of sweatshirt material (wrong-side-out) to the front of the sweatshirt.

3 Hand or machine stitch the rickrack on top of the edge of rectangle.

4 Hand or machine stitch the ball fringe to the bottom of the sweatshirt.

5 Arrange three stacks of two-buttons each on rectangle of fabric. When you are pleased with your arrangement, sew buttons in place using contrasting embroidery floss.

6 Using a running stitch, sew three concentric circles around the buttons in three different colors of embroidery floss (Fig. 1).

7 Sew the one remaining button on the outside of the rectangle. Using a contrasting embroidery thread, sew a circle around the button.

Fig. 1

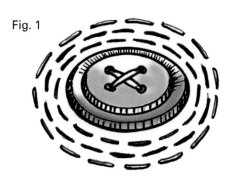

Pretty fabric posies, buttons and embroidery make this sweet girly sweatshirt a real favorite.

Pick-a-Posie Sweatshirt

{

Materials

1 child's sweatshirt

3 pieces complementary colored printed fabric

4 colors embroidery floss: 1 green, 3 colors to complement fabric.

1 yard of ball fringe

3 buttons

Tool Box

Scissors

Needle

Optional: Sewing machine

}

1 Turn the sweatshirt inside-out. The sweatshirt will be worn inside-out. Cut the waistband off of the sweatshirt.

2 Hand or machine sew the ball fringe to bottom of sweatshirt.

3 Hand-cut three different sized circles, slightly larger than the buttons, one from each piece of fabric. Make the circles slightly lop-sided for a more whimsical appearance.

4 Arrange fabric circles on the front of the sweatshirt in a pleasing manner. Pin in place.

5 Using embroidery floss, sew a spiral from the center of fabric circle to the outer edge (Fig. 1).

6 Sew straight stitches around the perimeter of the circle (Fig. 2).

7 Sew the buttons on with contrasting embroidery floss.

8 Using green embroidery floss, sew stems and leaves on the flowers (Fig. 3).

Fig. 1

Fig. 2

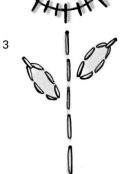

Fig. 3

Have a very merry holiday in this darling Christmas tree sweatshirt.

Trim-a-Tree Sweatshirt

{
Materials
1 child's sweatshirt
1 5"x 8" piece of sweatshirt fabric
1 triangle of green sweatshirt fabric for body of tree
1 yard ball fringe
9 green mother-of-pearl buttons
Gold seed beads
7 bugle beads for star and center of buttons
Gold/brown and green embroidery floss
Thread to match rectangle, tree and ball fringe

Tool Box
Scissors
Needle
Optional: Sewing machine
}

1 Turn the sweatshirt inside-out. The sweatshirt will be worn inside-out. Cut the waistband off of the sweatshirt.

2 Hand or machine sew the rectangle to the front of the sweatshirt.

3 Hand or machine sew the ball fringe to the bottom of the sweatshirt.

4 Hand or machine sew the tree triangle to the rectangle.

5 Using the gold/brown embroidery floss outline the tree with straight stitches. Sew the tree trunk using the same floss (Fig. 1).

6 Using the green embroidery floss outline rectangle with straight stitches (Fig.2).

7 Randomly sew the green mother-of-pearl buttons to tree, using gold seed beads in the center of the buttons.

8 Use the bugle beads and the remaining seed beads to make the star at the top of the tree (Fig. 3).

Fig. 1

Fig. 2

Fig. 3

Fashion Apparel

Add style and interest to a solid cardigan sweater with fabric and button detail. The design adapts easily to a zipper- or button-front sweater.

Double Placket Button Sweater

Materials

Solid color cardigan sweater-button front or zipper front.

6" x 24" piece cotton fabric--solid or small print

22 1/2" buttons

26 3/4" buttons

Hook and eye closures if sweater is not a zipper-front cardigan.

Thread for placket and buttons

Tool Box

Scissors

Needle

Iron

1 If the sweater has a zipper front, then skip to step 2. If the sweater has buttons, remove the buttons. Sew hook and eyes behind the center-front placket so they are not visible when the sweater is closed.

2 Cut 2 strips 2 -3/4" wide and the length of your sweater placket, plus 1" long. You can either cover the entire front sweater placket or expose the upper and/or lower ribbing on your sweater.

3 Fold under 1/2" on all four sides of the two fabric strips. Press flat with an iron. Pin the fabric to sweater fronts making sure that the folded fabric edge meets at the center fronts and upper and lower edges. Carefully slipstitch the fabric strips in place, close to the edge, using small even stitches.

4 Arrange the buttons on the cotton plackets in your design or follow our pattern. Cluster the buttons in groups of 2 or 3 and space some individual buttons randomly. Arrange some of the buttons to extend over the edge of the fabric and onto the sweater for added interest.

5 Stabilize your button design by using a small amount of fabric glue on the back of each button. Keep the button holes clear of glue.

6 Stitch the buttons in place using a thread color that coordinates with the buttons, fabric, and sweater.

7 Cut a rectangular piece of the cotton 5" x 6". Fold under the edges 1/4" and press with an iron. Place on the back of the sweater just above the left shoulder blade. Pin and slip-stitch in place. Embellish with buttons.

Resources

On the following pages we have listed the individual buttons from JHB International that were used in this book by their project name and page number. Where we have used vintage buttons, they are from the designer's own collection and many of the styles are being introduced in a Button Ware line of reproduction buttons. JHB International is one of the largest button suppliers in the world and is known for high quality, unique designs. The company is a compliment to Amy's creative vision. For more information about the individual buttons and to view the buttons online, visit the JHB website at www.buttons.com or call 800-525-9007.

Indygo Junction carries the full line of Button Ware kits and buttons at www.indygojunction.com as well as other supplies necessary to complete the projects in this book.

Stacked Elastic Bracelet
Page 10:
40180
40182
40183
40185
40187
40188
Page 11: Vintage

Vertical Stacked Elastic Bracelet
Page 12:
43152
43153
43154
42056
43155
43158
53069
53093

Ribbon Bracelet
Page 13:
Black/Blue:
14458
30061
53207

Brown:
33001
53216

Waxed Linen Bracelet
Page 14 Left to Right
#1 Asian Inspired:
15616
18509
31625
70502
72025
72046
90116

#2 Natural:
12942
53226
70500
70502
80385
84881
90056

#3 Red/Black:
15616
20189
31625
34201
70502
90655

#4: Vintage
Bottom Photo: Vintage

Shanked Button Elastic Bracelet
Page 16:
10122

10124
30473
30554
30763
31177
32646

Page 17: Vintage

Button Disk-Loop Bracelet
Page 19: Left to Right
#1: Vintage

#2 Mother-of-Pearl:
53223
70011
70024
70063
70067
70076
70081
70082
70086
70230
70311
70561
71893
71922
71926

#3 Colorful:
19584
19585
19586

19587
24052
43191
43193
49194
49196
49197

Charmingly Graceful
Page 20
Pink:
1010
1019
1022
1043
1060
14480
14483
24004
70086
70500

Mother-of-Pearl:
11260
15445
70006
70082
70557
71883
71889
71897

Charmingly Simple
Page 22, 23:
30119
37507
37517
53282
53283
53293
90283
91038
91161
91170
92077
92079
92322
92351
95098
95099

Stacked Beaded Bracelet
Page 25: Left to Right:
#1: Vintage

#2 Black/White:
10785
12377
12604
14458
15616
19234
31625
32115
32125
52332
53223
53224
70008
70502
71934

Visit JHB's website, www.buttons.com

#3: Vintage

#4: Vintage

Fabric Cuff
Page 27:
70500
70502
70505

Mother-of-Pearl Wire Choker
Page 31
Main Photo, Flower Drop:
11290
53223
53224

Top Right, Engraved Drop:
11290
53225

Bottom Right, Snowflake:
14454
70086
71930

Basic Stacked Pendant
Page 33
Main Photo:
32108
32607
53125
Clasp 963

Top Right: Vintage

Middle Right:
902
40173
53021
53391

Nature's Touch Pendant
Page 35:
40185
50043
50476
50812
53236
80331
80571
83099
96200

Bright And Sassy Pendant
Page 37:
18225
40779
40780
43186
43192
43196
43197
47314
53020
53507

Vineyard Pendant
Page 39:
11882
11893
19575
38254
43192
43193
45159
53021
84114

Christmas Tree Necklace
Page 41
Main Photo:
10423
10433
14036
40162
70805
93350

Side Photo: Vintage

Crochet Beaded Button Pendant
Page 43:
Mother-of-Pearl:
53206
53211
70024
70027
71220

Natural:
53206
53220
53228
70806
80242
80385
80571

Button Collage Necklace
Page 45:
12250
12270
40183
53098
53104
70258
70551
80385
80324
80325
80391
80548
80521
83913

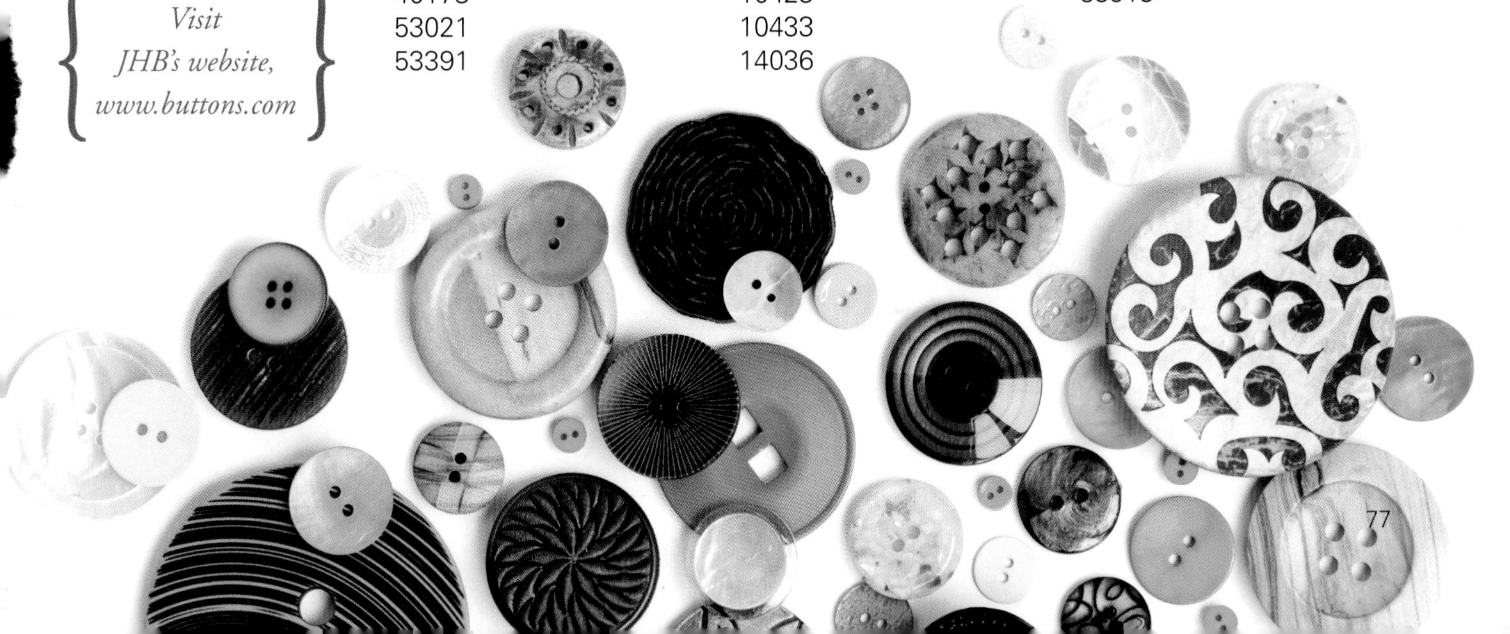

Beaded Button Pin
Page 51
Main Photo:
14458
15342
71922

Bottom Row
Left: Vintage

Middle:
14041
23416
38441
83555
Right: Vintage

Button Bouquet
Page 53
Main Photo: Vintage
Bottom Left: Vintage

Right:
18226
19585
30248
33032
36614

Flower Pin
Page 55
Main Photo: Vintage

Bottom Row Left:
40172
43184

Right:
12241
43193
53070

Stacked Button Pin
Page 56:
Diagonal:
32135
33041

Black/Orange:
10944
15340
19575
83554
85647

Brown/Maroon Oval:
33042
53125
80380
82935

Bobbys and Barrettes
Page 57:
Colorful:
19575
19576
38441
38442
38444

Mother-of-Pearl:
32081
11764
18226
53212
70007
71922

Elastic Button Ring
Page 58: Left to Right
Black/Silver:
14111
15449
35847

Multi:
31051
83751

Black/Orange:
10008
36614
43193

Tortoise:
11191
33031
84881

Far Right: Vintage

Wire Button Ring
Page 59: Left to Right:
Mother-of-Pearl: Vintage

Blue/Green:
14650
40163

Blue Mother-of-Pearl:
32081
53219
70076

Grey Mother-of-Pearl:
71368

Black Stripe:
19409
47317
70807

Recycled Heart Sweater
Page 63: Vintage

Button Spray Tee
Page 64:
70013
70500
70502
70689
70745
70814
70815
70861
71981
71988
71989
71979

Contemporary Cross
Page 65:
53210
70500
70502

Conversational Heart Tee
Page 67:
90441
90661
92112
94313
96205

Rickrack Abstract
Sweatshirt
Page 69:
38443
43184
43181
43186
43191
43193

Pick-a-Posie Sweatshirt
Page 71:
10432
40173
43194

Trim-a-Tree Sweatshirt
Page 73:
70805
70815

Double Placket Button
Sweater
Page 75:
71242
71243
71244
71246
71247
71248
71249
71261
71262
71263
71264
71266
71269

JHB ⠃⠌

Acknowledgments

This book has been a labor of love, and I have many to thank for fulfilling my vision for this title. My passion for collecting vintage buttons and the inspiring designs from so many talented artists led me down the path to create this book. JHB stepped in with their support, offering the source for buttons that are superior in quality and design. Robin Mackintosh agreed to lead the endeavor with her original design work as well as contributing designs based on my creative direction. She also assisted in our editing process. Jean Lowe brought her publishing experience and Kayte Price designed the book and styled the photography with photographer Darryl Bernstein. Secely Palmer added technical editing and Mary Ann Donze contributed the illustrations. Thanks to everyone.

To Jay Barr and the team at JHB International—Jean Barr, Lisa Lambright, Barbara Barr, Lynita Haber, Genevieve Ferguson, Ingrid Chernet—thank-you for your enthusiasm, support, and commitment to Button Ware.

A special thanks to Robin Mackintosh for her beautiful designs and involvement on every level throughout the development and editing process. It has been a joy to work with you!

Special thanks to the following designers for their projects featured in this book.

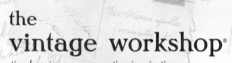

80